OPERATION QUICKSILVER

PETER TOOLEY

IAN HENRY PUBLICATIONS

The illustrations on the cover are of
'Bigbobs' moored in the Beaulieu River
and of
A genuine LCT in operation off Sicily

British Library Cataloguing in Publication Data

Tooley, Peter
    Operation Quicksilver.
    1. World War 2. Military operations by
    Allied forces. Strategy. Deceptions
    I. Title
    940.54'012

ISBN 0-86025-415-1

Printed by
View Publications (Bristol), Ltd.
Arnolds Fields Estate, Wickwar, Gloucestershire GL12 8NP
for
Ian Henry Publications, Ltd.
20 Park Drive, Romford, Essex RM1 4LH

PREFACE

Since the days of the Trojan Horse deception has been a potent weapon of war. The biggest bluff in the history of armed conflict was mounted by the Allied Forces in the run-up to 'D-day' during World War II. A massive operation codenamed *Fortitude* was designed to mislead the German High Command as to the time and place of the European invasion. Part of this operation, stretching from Norway to Gibraltar, involved the building of a dummy fleet of ships. 'Operation *Quicksilver*' tells the full story of this phantom fleet for the first time, from its inception until its final deployment in the invasion summer of 1944.

AIR MINISTRY,

c/o GPO SHEPPETON.

MIDDLESEX.

C.T./P/NO.2

29th March, 1943.

Dear Dunlop

1.   I am getting on with the dummy L.C.T. and have come. to the state in which I must send people down to look at the original to see what fittings to add to make it lifelike. I should think in about ten days time it ought to be finished, but there are one or two little mistakes to remedy so that it will not be perfect.

2.   I have contacted the Experimental Bridging Establishment at CHRISTCHURCH and one of their officers has been up to view the dummy. He is of the opinion that it should be sufficiently stable, but he considers that it will take a considerable time to re-erect when such action is needed. He believes that it would be quite easy to prepare a lighter and more easily erected design at the Experimental Bridging Establishment, but I cannot give him authority to go ahead with this. He is in no doubt about success in the matter. He admits that his pattern will take more labour to construct because it will be made largely of wooden sections. On the other hand these sections will fit together quickly when the time comes for erection. If, therefore the B.G.S. thinks fit I suggest that the Establishment be asked to push through another type dummy as soon as possible.

3.   It is unfortunate that they were not asked before. I have tried to contact them myself for over a month but they have always stated that they were too busy to send up an officer to look at the dummy and give advice.

When I have finished my pattern I will let you know and have photographs taken.

I am contacting the Navy to obtain the details I mentioned above.

Yours sincerely,

(SGD) J.F. TURNER

When are you going to have another meeting. Even if no decision in detail can be given as to our activities, a practice reconnaissance is vitally urgent and long overdelayed.

Lieutenant Colonel A. Dunlop,
   G.H.Q. Home Forces.

"Prior to D-day the plan was to indicate to the enemy that the assault was to be delivered in the Pas de Calais, astride Cap Gris Nez. After D-day, our objective was to show that the *Neptune* assault was a preliminary and diversionary operation designed to draw German reserves away from the Pas de Calais and Belgium and that our main attack was still to be delivered in the Pas de Calais.

Large numbers of dummy landing craft were assembled in ports in south-east England where dummy hard-standings, full-scale embarkation sign-posting and other visible signs of preparation were made obvious. American and Canadian troops were moved into the Dover-Folkestone area to lend credence to the idea.

These deception measures continued as planned after D-day and events were to show that they achieved outstanding results and in fact played a vital part in our successes in Normandy."

NORMANDY TO THE BALTIC
Field-Marshal Lord Montgomery

Subject: Dummy Landing Craft

Army Ops Branch (US)

2 July, 1943.

Reference "Recommendations for use of Dummy Landing Craft" issued 21st June, 1943.

STORAGE OF DUMMY CRAFT

1.   The transportation of the Bigbob assemblies presents a big problem, inasmuch as one Bigbob requires eight 3-ton trucks or three 10-ton railway wagons. It is, therefore, necessary that a storage site for the seventy-five dummy craft required for AMERICAN operations in 1943 be selected as early as possible, so that the craft can be delivered from the factory as complete assemblies become ready for issue. Will you, therefore, please take action in accordance with para.22(f) of the above quoted recommendations.

TRAINING OF TEAMS FOR ERECTION OF BIGBOBS

2.   Experiments have shown that one Bigbob takes 18 trained men six hours to erect.

3.   It is estimated that team leaders will require three weeks training to become thoroughly acquainted with the various parts of the dummy craft and the methods of assembly.   The remainder of the team will require a minimum of one week's training.

4.   As only one prototype is available for training it will be necessary to co-ordinate the training of AMERICAN and BRITISH teams, and it is suggested that ETOUSA be requested to arrange direct with GHQ, Home Forces (21 Army Group when formed) for the combined training of teams of both Army Groups.

(SGD) H. BUCHANAN-DUNLOP Lt.-Col.
for MGGS

Army Ops Branch (BRIT)

Copies to:- The Under Secretary of State,
          The War Office (WV2)

          General Headquarters,
             Home Forces (for 21 Army Group)

THE MECHANICAL ELEPHANT

During the ominous calm of the early months of World War II the War Cabinet decided to set up a secret deception unit to be master-minded by Sir John Turner, who was Director of Works at the Air Ministry. A retired Army officer of great drive and initiative, Sir John was charged with the task of devising clandestine operations to mislead and confuse the enemy. By the summer of 1940 'Turner's Circus' had constructed a number of dummy airfields in the Home Counties known as 'K' sites. These were provided with plywood aircraft and hangars which had been fabricated in film-studio workshops at Elstree and elsewhere. At night simulated flarepaths and huge fires, known as *Starfish,* were used in the open countryside to divert enemy bombers from their targets.

The success of such operations during the summer of 1940 at the time of the Battle of Britain encouraged the use of similar deception tactics by General Wavell in the North African desert campaigns of 1941-2. A group known as A-force, under the command of Brigadier Dudley Clarke, effectively deployed numbers of rubber inflatable tanks and vehicles called *Bagpipes* to beguile enemy intelligence.

The Royal Navy experimented with the notion of modifying old merchant ships to resemble war-ships, which might be used to lure enemy ships and aircraft within gun range. In the event only three of these 'Q' ships were built and they were eventually laid up, never having been used. However, the Navy was soon to be involved in another secret operation, known as *Quicksilver,* which eventually played an important part in the success of the Normandy landings in 1944.

At a meeting on a wet January morning in 1943 the Allied Chiefs-of-Staff finally decided to postpone *Roundup,* the proposed invasion of Europe in the summer of that year. It was agreed, however, that a number of deception operations should be mounted to keep the German High Command on their toes. A few days later at a meeting of Roundup Sub-Committee 3, John Turner was asked to explore the possibility of building a fleet of dummy landingcraft in collaboration with the Army Camouflage Development and Training School based at Farnham Castle, Surrey. Although mainly concerned with camouflage, the Farnham School was also experienced in the training of Royal Engineer deception groups, known as 'R' force. Appropriately one of the School's staff officers at that time was a son of the famous cartoonist, William Heath Robinson.

The dummy craft were intended to be deployed along the South Coast with the object of pinning down enemy troops across the Channel and diverting attention from real operations taking place in the run-up to D-day, now planned for the summer of 1944. A number of engineering firms were to be approached under conditions of great secrecy and asked to submit designs for the decoy ships. The craft had to be suitable for use in estuaries and coastal waters and able to withstand a Force 4 wind. They also had to be capable of construction within a space of 8 hours, so that they could be built and launched during the hours of darkness.

At this time all deception planning was brought under the jurisdiction of Colonel John Bevan, an ex-stockbroker with a Military Medal from the first World War and a reputation for cutting red tape and getting things done. Within a few weeks he had built up the nucleus of what became known as 'Devices Branch', a section of the Joint Planning Staff based in London's Cadogan Square.

One of the firms contacted by Devices Branch was Cox & Co., an engineering works on the outskirts of Watford. In February the Managing Director, Howard Wilton, received a mysterious telephone call from a Colonel Alferoff, asking if the company would be prepared to collaborate on the design and manufacture of a product of considerable importance to the war effort. Alferoff refused to give any further details, but invited Wilton and his chief design engineer, Chris Toon, to Cadogan Square later in the month. Following this meeting the Watford factory was visited by Captain Johnson Marshall, who had been appointed to deal with design matters. In great confidence he outlined the nature and purpose of the dummy craft to Wilton and Toon.

That night Toon was already at his drawing board and, after several weeks of discussion and innumerable drawings, a broad specification was decided upon. The ship was to resemble a Landing Craft (Tank) Mark 4, a vessel of about 31' beam and 175' long with 400 tons displacement. The hull was to be constructed of $3\frac{1}{4}$" steel tubing to form an articulated raft floating on a number of sealed metal drums. To permit rapid assembly the tubes were connected using fish plates and metal cotter pins. This produced a bridgelike structure of great strength on the principle of the Warren Girder, which had been used successfully in the design of the Hawker Hurricane fighter plane.

To this cantilever-type hull were bolted welded fabrications to give the correct flare and shape of the ship's sides, bow and stern. The metal skeleton was then covered with sheets of painted canvas, fastened together with laces and eyelets. Duckboards served as decking and the deck housing, bridge, funnel and bow doors were to be built up from prefabricated units. Dimensions were to be exactly as the real LCT and the parts transportable in 3-ton trucks or railway wagons. In addition, the flotation cradles were fitted with stub axles holding iron wheels, to enable transportation for short distances overland.

To maintain secrecy the prototype was erected in a plastic blister hangar built for this purpose in the factory car park. Only the hull of the craft was assembled and Troon, with a whimsical sense of humour, put it about that he was building a mechanical elephant. The next stage was to carry out floatation tests and, after some local reconnaissance, it was decided to use Frensham Great Pond, just outside Farnham. In due course the main cantilever, about 150' long and weighing 4 tons, was successfully launched after being assembled on the adjacent Common. The whole structure was supported on six floats each consisting of three empty 45-gallon oil drums and proved to be remarkably stable.

On 29th March, 1943, John Turner wrote to Colonel Dunlop, GHQ Home Forces, reporting on the initial success of the flotation tests. With the addition of one or two fittings suggested by the Navy to make it more lifelike, he thought the prototype should be ready to undergo its sea trials in about ten days.

An officer from the Experimental Bridging Establishment at Christchurch, who had been at the Frensham trials, was not convinced, however, that Troon's model could be assembled within the required time limit, although he was impressed by the stability of the craft in the water. He was certain that the EBE could design a much lighter model made of wood. Although this would take more labour to construct it would fit together more quickly when the time came for erection.

Turner recommended that permission be given for them to push through their plans for a wooden dummy as soon as possible, although he was a little peeved that it had not been suggested before. 'It is unfortunate they were not asked before,' he commented, 'but I have tried to contact them myself for over a month and they have always stated that they were too busy to send up an officer to look at the dummy and give advice'.

Action followed swiftly and the Experimental Bridging team were invited to take their model, when completed, to Lepe at the mouth of the River Beaulieu in Hampshire, where Toon's model was to undergo its sea trials during April. Writing to Colonel Dunlop again on 6th April, Turner thanked him for expediting action on the EBE model and inviting him to come and see Toon's craft on the following Monday. He also took the opportunity to underline his feelings about the importance of decoy operations in modern warfare.

'I feel that far too little is known of the decoy system in this country,' he complained, 'Naturally, we have kept our mouths shut about it. I feel, however, the time has come in which those responsible for laying down policy should know of the possibilities of this weapon and what it has achieved in the past. My reason is that I consider that decoys can be used not only strategically in this country to induce the enemy to keep his reserves well away from our point of attack, but also in the early stages of forming a bridgehead when we do attack.

'I thoroughly understand that shipping and craft well be used to the utmost in getting over vital interests in the form of food, ammunition, etc., and that very little will be available for decoy work. My point is that until the powers that be accept the decoy as a weapon none will be available; with the result that decoys, if sent out, will be too late to draw off attack in the early stages when they will be most effective.'

Meanwhile, arrangements had been made for a small team of Cox's employees to travel down to Lepe with their model. Accordingly, John English, who had been appointed Field Officer for the trials, and Jim Clay, from the production side at Cox's, set out from the Watford factory in a small van filled with gear to set up camp at the test site. Clay recalls how they scoured the beach to find a suitably secluded spot for their purpose. Finally they settled on a smooth, gently shelving patch of sand, close by a small wood.

Being a master builder by trade he soon set about knocking up some rough bench seats and tables, using some recently felled timber lying nearby. To finish off his efforts, he finally climbed a large fir tree overlooking the camp and nailed a board to the trunk, which was inscribed with 'Cox's Holiday Camp'. At the same time, English had been busy erecting some tentlike shelters by throwing tarpaulins over conveniently situated tree branches and then pegging them to the ground using metal spikes. After all had been made ready they returned to the factory.

Within a few days they were back with a task force of about twenty uniformed Cox's employees under the command of Major E H Wilton all members of the 20th Company, Middlesex Home

Guard, the factory security force. Accompanying them was a small convoy of lorries and trailers, carrying an assortment of steel tubing and other stores required to build the dummy craft.

After a short time at the 'Robinson Crusoe' camp, it was decided to billet the men in Lepe House, a large timbered mansion overlooking The Solent, which at one time had belonged to the Sitwell family. This move greatly eased the catering problems and was particularly welcomed by John English as it came under the jurisdiction of the Navy and enabled him to get supplies of duty free pipe tobacco!

The following year Lepe was to become a major assembly point for landing craft sailing to the Normandy beaches. A concrete hard and slip was built on the beach between Lepe House and White House, which remains to this day. In addition the road from Lepe to Langley was widened and strengthened to take tanks and other heavy vehicles, while tank traps were cut into the cliff near Nelson's Place in Stanswood Bay.

For security reasons, only the main frame of the model was to be built for the flotation tests, without the bow and stern sections, the bridge, deckhouse or funnel. Construction work was started at low tide and was finished within a few hours. Unfortunately, when the tide came in the weight of the steel skeleton caused it to sink deeply into the soft, wet sand and, despite the efforts of the beach party, who were by this time waist deep in water, the structure refused to budge. Just as they were at their wits' end as to what to do next a party of soldiers appeared, doubling along the beach. The officer in charge, seeing their plight, ordered his men to lend a hand and soon the craft was afloat to the accompaniment of ironic cheers from the launching party.

However, the relief of getting it away safely soon turned to dismay as it drifted quite quickly out to sea with about nine of the launching party still aboard, perched perilously on the narrow scaffolding. The remainder of the party was sent off in search of help from the Navy or any of the locals who owned boats. Eventually the Navy came to the rescue with a small tug and towed the craft back to the beach, where it was securely fastened to mooring stakes driven into the sand. Several of the men had to be sent to hospital suffering from exposure after this incident, as they were subjected to the icy spray and wind while dressed only in swimming trunks.

Shortly afterwards a small group of Service and civilian 'boffins' arrived and, after making a detailed inspection of the floating vessel, left to make their report. The structure was then dismantled and taken back to Watford.

Cox's factory, Watford, today

BIGBOB TAKES SHAPE

Several other designs were considered, including that submitted by the Experimental Bridging Establishment. Most appeared to be designed around standard pontoon sections, however, and were cumbersome and far less stable than Toon's model. Eventually it was decided unanimously to adopt the Cox's pattern and further sea trials were ordered immediately. English and his party were soon back at Lepe and what followed is best described in his own words –

The structure was to be towed out to sea to see what effect wave motion would have on its stablity. Accordingly, next day a small Naval tug took the device in tow with Chris Toon and myself clinging precariously to the structural members in order that we could study the effects of stress on the design. We skirted the west coast of the Isle of Wight and were taken about four miles into the English Channel, when the tug developed engine trouble and promptly cast us adrift, leaving us to our own devices for a couple of hours, until another tug appeared to tow us back to Lepe, I remember that, while adrift, we appeared to be moving quite rapidly towards the French coast – probably only imagination. During this time an aeroplane arrived and circled round us at such a height that we could not determine its identity. I remember Chris and I deciding that if it came any closer we would dive into the 'drink', but, fortunately, after circling a few times, it disappeared. The device came through all tests with flying colours and, after spending a few days at Lepe developing the assembly drill, we returned to the factory. As a matter of interest, while I was at Lepe I took the opportunity of visiting Buckler's Hard, where many of the ships of the line were built in Nelson's day. This was of particular interest to me as my family on my mother's side were the largest wooden ship builders in the U.K. until World War I, based at Lowestoft in Suffolk.

Toon and English had a further misadventure a few days later, when the dummy broke away from its moorings one evening with the two of them aboard. Luckily by this time the craft had been fitted with a small Petter marine engine and they were able, after a few anxious moments, to manoeuvre alongside an anchored Naval vessel. After tying up they spent the night drinking rum with the Captain and listening to his views on idiots who spent their time drifting in the Solent at night, without lights, on Heath Robinson contraptions.

There were still some lingering doubts as to the wisdom of committing men and materials to this particular deception exercise and Colonel Bevan was asked to lend his authority to convince the sceptics at HQ. On 15th April, 1943 he despatched a secret letter from the London office of the War Cabinet in Great George Street addressed to Brigadier Buchanan of Home Forces planning HQ endorsing Turner's views on the importance of the deception plan.

While surplus real craft would be preferable

to implement the cover plan, it was highly unlikely that these would be available for some time and he felt convinced that any deception plan concerned with amphibious operations based on this country, would entail the employment of numerous dummy landing craft of various descriptions. He reported that, during the previous three weeks, he had seen Colonel Dudley Clarke in Algiers, who had advanced a considerable way towards contructing dummy LCT's for use in the Mediterranean. Accordingly, he had requested specifications for these craft be sent immediately to the U.K. for their information.

His exasperation at the Admiralty's lack of enthusiasm for the project is clearly shown. 'It seems to me,' he complains, 'that when the experts have decided on the best types of dummy craft they can construct, somebody has got to give an order for their construction in large numbers. In the past the Admiralty have, I believe, expressed the view that shortages of material and manpower were the main factors against the construction of dummy craft, especially LCTs. I do feel, however, that these might be surmounted if some high authority gave a definite order that the craft had got to be constructed.'

Subsequent events show that his plea did not go unheeded and instructions were given at the highest level for work on the dummy craft to be given priority.

By now Toon and English had returned to Watford with their team and work was completed on the details of superstructure and deck fittings. A full scale assembly exercise was planned to be carried out in the presence of a small group of senior Army officers and NCOs, selected from units who would eventually supply the erection and launch teams. The problem was to find a

12

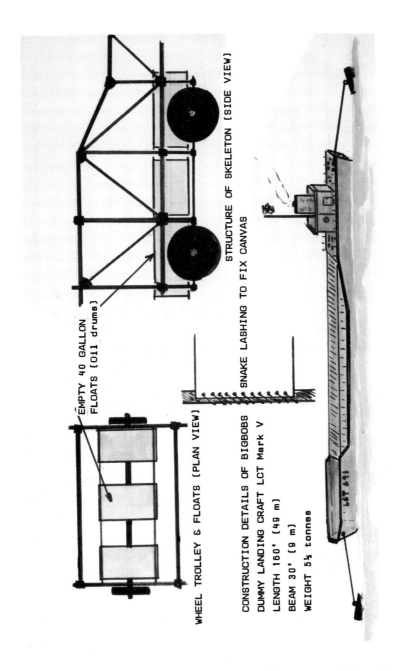

WHEEL TROLLEY & FLOATS (PLAN VIEW)

EMPTY 40 GALLON FLOATS (Oil drums)

STRUCTURE OF SKELETON (SIDE VIEW)

SNAKE LASHING TO FIX CANVAS

CONSTRUCTION DETAILS OF BIGBOBS
DUMMY LANDING CRAFT LCT Mark V
LENGTH 160' (49 m)
BEAM 30' (9 m)
WEIGHT 5½ tonnes

convenient building in the London area, which was large enough to hold the fully assembled model and which was secure from prying eyes.

A disused warehouse off Scrubs Lane, close to Willesden Junction, was utilised to accommodate the first assembly, but eventually it was decided to use a former bus garage in Leysfield Road, Shepherd's Bush, which had been commandeered as an RAOC ordnance depot, commanded by Major Coleman. By early July all was ready and, using a team from the factory and under ideal conditions, it was found possible to carry out the assembly of the model in the remarkable time of 3 hours and 20 minutes. Understandably this record was unlikely to be repeated under field conditions in darkness, but it proved that the deadline of 8 hours building time could be met without a great deal of difficulty.

For security and convenience the dummy LCTs were now referred to as *Bigbobs* to differentiate them from small inflatable rubber dummy craft, which were termed *Wetbobs**.

The Bigbob assembly remained at the Leysfield Road garage until 6th July, when it was dismantled and taken back to the test site at Beaulieu. Here it was re-erected and moored next to a real LCT of the same appearance and photographed from the air at low level. The results were quite spectacular. The only way of telling the vessels apart was that the dummy looked too clean. This was remedied by liberally splashing sump oil over the sides and superstructure and painting rust marks in appropriate places.

Meanwhile, back at Cox's factory production was moving into top gear. Elements of the RAOC, in the charge of Lieutenant Reader and Sergeant

* The origin of these names may be traced back to Eton School, where the term 'wetbob' is used to describe a boating enthusiast.

French, were moved in to handle the storage of completed assemblies and their despatch to operational sites when these had been selected. Since it had been decided that at least 75 craft would be wanted, large areas of hard-standing adjacent to the works were set aside as temporary open-air dumps. Additional floor space was also urgently required in the factory itself, a problem finally resolved by building a number of additional plastic hangars in the grounds.

All welding, painting and finishing was carried out in the hangars, the rivetting, pressing and machining operations being performed in the works. Transportation of the finished assemblies from the factory was also a headache, as each Bigbob needed 8 Army 3-ton trucks or three 10-ton railway wagons. Reproduced by permission of the Public Record Office

A real LCT Mark IV moored alongside a Bigbob in the River Beaulieu. The Bigbob (left) looked too clean and had to be 'dirtied' using sump oil

VIRGINIA WATER and BUCKLER'S HARD

It was now necessary to establish an inland site for training the erection teams. Each squad was to consist of 18 men, in the charge of an NCO acting as team leader. These leaders were to be given a threeweek course to enable them to be sufficiently acquainted with the various parts of the dummy craft to be able to check all the components and stores before assembly. The rest of the team would receive a minimum of a week's training.

The site selected had to be reasonably close to Cox's Watford factory and to the Camouflage Development and Training Centre at Farnham, which was to oversee the operation. It also had to be possible to debar the public from access to the site and prevent any view of the proceedings by unauthorised persons. Small motor boats were also needed to help in the launching and mooring of the Bigbobs, while the RE were asked to offer some form of dimmed lighting for use on moonless nights.

Two possible locations were considered; Hawley Lake, situated on a common $1\frac{1}{2}$ miles from Sandhurst and Virginia Water, an articifical lake some $1\frac{1}{2}$ miles long, in the south east corner of Windsor Great Park: the latter was eventually chosen as being far superior from the security point of view. Being in one of the Royal Parks, however, meant that permission had to be sought from King George VI to use it.

Additionally, Mr Saville, the Chief Agent for Crown Lands, was required to vouch for the integrity of the 30 workers on the Royal Estate. A strict security ban was enforced over the whole area, which was cordoned off by the Military Police. Sole access to the site was by means of a small gate at the side of the Wheatsheaf Hotel.

Despite all precautions, a serious breach of security occurred on the very first day of the exercise, 14th July, although it verged on the farcical. Just before operations commenced a security guard spotted a couple in close embrace on a small islet right in front of the launch point. A boat was sent out to apprehend them and questioning revealed that they were both married, but not to each other. Naturally, they were concerned at the outcome of their indiscretion and feared the worst. However, the officer in charge of security was a compassionate man and they were allowed to depart in peace, after swearing not to disclose anything they had seen.

This ludicrous event was an omen of further troubles. The Army had decided that the Bigbob operation was not a task technical enough to warrant the use of Royal Engineers. Accordingly, the job was allocated to two companies of the Pioneer Corps, under the command of Lieutenant-Colonel Peter White of 24th Airfield Construction Group.

John English, who had been appointed as Cox's representative on the site, was far from happy. In his report he wrote:

> I regret to say the whole exercise resulted in a most ghastly fiasco. Neither the officers nor the men seemed to have any idea of what was required of them. After a few days hard

work, I began to despair of making any progress. Indeed, their Commanding Officer virtually accused me of telling untruths in stating that the device could be erected in under eight hours. Finally, when in the middle of erecting the funnel assembly, perhaps the most difficult part, a whistle was blown and the men just dropped everything, the assembly collapsing with me underneath it. After making a rather undignified exit from the shambles, I enquired the reason for blowing the whistle. I was told it was time for the men to have a swim! I at once packed up and returned to the factory where I reported the circumstance to Col. White.

These teething problems were soon overcome and, after two weeks spent in erecting and dismantling Bigbobs, the men entered fully into the spirit of things and became quite expert, even when operating in the dark. The teams eagerly competed against each other and the building time was rapidly reduced. In due course the Pioneers were followed at the training site by an American Army engineering unit, who also worked with great enthusiasm and ultimately achieved a record assembly time of just over three hours.

The War Office arranged for another company of American Engineers, under the command of Captain Mackie, to handle the subassembly work at Cox's and be responsible for the storage and dispatch of Bigbob parts to the chosen operational sites. This released RAOC personnel working at the factory for transfer to the Central Ordnance Depot at Elstree. Here a special 'hospital' was set up for the repair of dummy craft which had been damaged by weather or enemy action. By this time John English had been commissioned into the RAOC and was appointed officer-in-charge of the

Elstree workshops.

Plans were now finalised by General Sir Frederick Morgan, Chief-of-Staff to the Supreme Allied Commander (COSSAC), for about 80 Bigbobs to be launched and moored at various sites along the South Coast. These were to be located in sheltered isolated spots, having gently sloping beaches and adjacent land suitable for storage and assembly.

The selection and survey of suitable sites was carried out by Captain Johnson Marshall, who had already been involved in the original trials at Buckler's Hard. In consultation with Captain Luce, RN, of Portsmouth Command, it was decided to use secluded stretches of beach in the harbours of Poole, Dartmouth and Falmouth, Buckler's Hard near Beaulieu, and East Hard adjacent to West Wittering at the mouth of Chichester Harbour. The American Engineers were to be responsible for the launches in Devon and Cornwall, while the Pioneers would operate the other sites.

Meeting at Wilton House, near Salisbury, on 16th July, the planners decided that a series of launches would commence with 8 craft at Falmouth on 12th August. During the following week seven further craft would be launched at Dartmouth and 36 at Poole on the following three nights. The final launch of another 24 craft would take place at Wittering and Buckler's Hard. This rolling programme enabled one group of American and British troops to carry out operations at Falmouth, Poole and West Wittering, while a second group worked at the remaining locations.

Each of the British groups comprised 12 construction teams of 20 men, together with a team leader who was either a junior officer or a senior NCO – a total of 500 men in all – from the 92nd and 214th Companies of the Pioneer Corps.

Colonel Peter White and the author outside Walnut Cottage, Benenden, 43 years after Quicksilver (inset: The author as boat officer of 446 Flotilla, Royal Marines at Woolverstone, 1944)

Surprisingly, it was only at this stage that the officers of the British and American teams met one another. Peter White remembers the occasion well:

> My Field Engineer and I went to meet our American opposite numbers. What a cheerful crowd they were! They were a bit diffident about dealing with senior British Naval Officers, so I went with them to explain our wants to the SNOs at Falmouth and Plymouth. It was there that I met those magnificent Admirals of the Fleet and retired Admirals who, masquerading as Captains and Commanders, were manning the Staffs of these ports. I rather thought that they did not much approve of our escapade, but they gave us all the help we needed. It was in Plymouth that we stayed for a night in a hostel run by two charming American ladies. Here I enjoyed listening to American banter and learnt a lot about inter-State rivalry in the USA.

Another incident recalled by Colonel White was finding part of an old hard while clearing a way down the river at the Buckler's Hard site. This had undoubtedly been used some 150 years before to launch some of Nelson's men-of-war.

The Bigbob assemblies were transported by road, since rail transport was thought to involve too many changes. Construction timetables were linked to the movement of real LCTs along the South Coast to give the impression that the Bigbobs had arrived overnight in convoy.

Security at the launch sites was taken very seriously. In consultation with Colonel White, the Chief Constable of Hampshire instructed Lyndhurst divisional police to serve notice on all visitors to the Parish of Beaulieu requiring them to leave the area by Saturday, 14th August, at the latest. The Parish was divided into two zones: the outer zone included that part of the surrounding countryside from which launching and mooring operations could be seen, and the inner zone a small area from which the actual building of the craft would be visible. Movement in the outer zone was restricted to those persons having National Registration Cards carrying home addresses within Beaulieu village, while entry to the inner zone was only permitted to residents and bonafide tradesmen delivering essential supplies. These regulations come into effect at midnight on 15th August, when a postal and telephone censorship was also implemented.

The need for such Draconian measures arose from the fact that in addition to the Bigbob enterprise, Beaulieu had become a centre for a number of other secret activities. Notably it had become a base for the Special Operations Executive (S.O.E.), where agents were trained before being parachuted into Europe to help the Resistance. There was also a fighter airfield on Beaulieu Heath, near Hatchet Gate. A second airfield (Need's Ore) was under construction near the mouth of the Beaulieu Estuary at Park Farm. This was completed in February, 1944, and used as an advanced landing strip for Typhoons and Thunderbolts covering the D-day landings.

The security ban was particularly irksome to the young Lord Montagu of Beaulieu who, at the end of his summer term at Eton, had to obtain a special pass to visit his parents at Palace House.

One or two houses and the Master Builder's House actually overlooked the launch site and these received special attention. A report to operational HQ from the local Army Commander, dated 12th August, read:

The picquets and patrols to ensure these

measures being carried out have been closely discussed with the local police and the requirements are 30 additional military police from Command resources. Please say if these are available.

With regard to the restriction of view over the actual construction and launching point from the windows of the three houses that overlook it, arrangements have been made with Superintendent Appleton that he will, during the morning of 13th August, make detailed arrangements with the hotel and Major Baillie that Pioneer officers and/or other ranks or Military Police should be billeted in the rooms with offending windows in the hotel and the Harbourmaster's house. The intention is to keep these rooms locked during the time that the personnel billeted are not actually in occupation.

With regard to Mr Kenneth Moore's house, arrangements are being made by Superintendent Appleton that at 12.00 hours on 13th August the offending rooms shall be barricaded and rendered useless as view points during the period of this op.

With regard to the site at Poole (as in the case of Buckler's Hard), one field security sergeant living in and an attachment of Military Police have been provided directly under the control of the Pioneer Company command. A short length of the road at the Lakeside building and launching site will be closed forthwith and ample MP are provided for Major Lewis to ensure this being done. Directly facing the building site there is a row of bungalows which are, however, occupied by people well known to the Poole police and it is recommended that the opinion of the police in this connection be accepted. It is pointed out that more than one op of a MOST SECRET nature has been carried out from this site recently and it was therefore agreed with the CRE 24 Airfield Construction Group that the less the ostentation in the security arrangements, the more effective they would be.

As an additional precaution, the regular BOAC civilian flight from Poole was diverted to Hythe during the time of the operations. Records were also made of the passage of all enemy aircraft in the area. The coastal batteries and Royal Observer posts in the vicinity being asked to pass on information regarding all aircraft passing over sites at 30,000' or below. Aerial photos of the moored Bigbobs were then taken to ascertain what might be visible from the air.

The RAF also arranged to fly Colonel White over the construction sites containing partly-built skeletons. He reported that, although the tubular steel scaffolding provided no clue as to its purpose, the shape of a boat was clearly outlined by the tracks of the men walking round it. The Poole site gave no problems as it was on shingle. At Buckler's Hard, on grass, and at Wittering, on sand, there had to be a party raking and making deliberate crisscross tracks over the site. Even so, the outline of the dummy was never quite obliterated.

At Buckler's Hard the Bigbobs were towed by the Navy to buoys some ¾ mile downstream, close to Clobb's Copse. On the opposite side of the river in some old disused oyster beds the construction company, Wates, were building an experimental floating dock made of concrete. This was used as a prototype for the Mulberry harbour units used on D-day, some of which were built at Lepe by Mowlems. This posed further security problems,

Beaulieu village, looking down the main street

Reproduced by permission of the National Motor Museum

The Master Builder's House, Buckler's Hard, with the Beaulieu River in the background

as revealed in a further report from the local commander, dated 2nd September:

Most Secret   Notes on Security Measures - Beaulieu Area

1. Gate leading from field to edge of Dungehill Copse to be wired up and 'Keep Out' notice fixed.
2. Mr Smith of Fiddlers who has a close and uninterrupted view of the objects is fully aware of their nature.
3. In the Naval Establishment on the west bank, Messrs Wates Ltd (civilian contractors) employ civilian labourers who are not residents in the area. It is not known to what extent these have been vetted beyond the routine police check. So far as Phase 2 is concerned they have an excellent view at the present time.
4. During a recce made by Capt Howard of this HQ and Officer Commanding 302 Field Security Section the objects were examined at a distance of less than 300 yds from points on both sides of the river and at the time there was a considerable wind blowing. They reported that the billowing of the canvas was quite easily seen with the naked eye. As a result of this it has been considered necessary to increase the patrols during phase 11 to ensure that there is no possible chance of unauthorised persons obtaining a close view.

As was to be expected, until the construction crews got used to working together at night, there were a number of problems. There were also liaison problems with the Naval tug crews who had the task of towing the dummy craft off the hards and mooring them down river.

On 13th August an observer from 21st Army

Group HQ attended the night's operations at Buckler's Hard, when it was hoped to launch seven Bigbobs. On his arrival at the site just before 7 p.m., work had stopped for the time being to enable the Pioneers to have their evening meal. The evening was fine and clear, although a stiffish breeze had got up making the water rather choppy. However, the seven skeletons had almost been completed and were standing on the hard by the river edge. The funnels had not been erected and the canvas covering was still to be put on, so the structures were unrecognisable to any casual observers: as it happened there was nobody about at that time of night and the adjoining shipyard was deserted.

At 7.45 work was resumed on all the Bigbobs as Colonel White and Major Lewis, the Pioneer Company Commander, both insisted that an early start was essential if the building was to be finished by daybreak. The observer was concerned in case the nature of the craft became obvious before darkness fell and asked that the erection of the funnels and the canvas cladding should be put off until the last possible moment, consistent with the completion of the programme by dawn.

It began to get dark just after 9 o'clock and work on the funnels was started, the first being in position half an hour later. The construction teams worked on all the Bigbobs simultaneously and Major Lewis reported that the first craft would be ready for launching at approximately midnight. The Navy had estimated thtat it would take half an hour to launch and two away each Bigbob to the moorings down river, which would have allowed ample time for the whole operation to be completed on time. Unfortunately, this was the first time the teams had worked under field conditions and some of the components, which had arrived fresh from the factory a few days earlier, were faulty. Therefore the first Bigbob was not ready for launching until 2.50 a.m. and, by the time the Naval tugs had been alerted, a further twenty minutes had elapsed before it was under tow.

By this time work on the other Bigbobs was going well and catching up, but the trouble now was a bottleneck on the Naval side in getting the finished craft away to their moorings. Everything seemed fated to go awry and, in fact, the tugs did not tow away the second craft until 5 a.m.

By then it was obvious that the full programme of launches would not be possible before dawn and it was decided to cut the losses and tow away only three Bigbobs. The other four had to be partially dismantled by removing the funnels and covering, leaving only the bare skeletons visible. The last Bigbob was launched and safely moored by 6 a.m. and the remaining craft on shore had been stripped down and the parts removed and stowed away out of sight just before dawn broke. At this time there was still no sign of life in the adjacent shipyard.

Colonel White decided to re-erect and launch the four remaining Bigbobs on the following night, 14th August, so that his target of 15 launches could be achieved within three days. Although the night's work was disappointing in that less than half the programme was completed, the Bigbobs which had been launched stood up to the very choppy conditions afloat and looked completely realistic at their moorings.

The official observer was optimistic. 'The difficulties experienced on this first night,' he wrote, 'arose firstly from the material of the Bigbobs and inexperience of the labour for erecting them, and later from the Naval bottleneck in being able to launch and tow away only one Bigbob at a time, on a night when a strong wind and the tide made this a slow process. Col White hopes that on subsequent nights the erection will be quicker and that the Navy will provide two or possibly three pairs of tugs, in which case there should be no difficulty in completing the programmes on time.'

Despite all the problems there were still some light-hearted moments and Peter White recalls how, at Wittering for the launching of the last craft, a bottle of beer was broken over its bows. It left the beach with the OC 92nd Pioneer Company, Major 'Max' Lewis, wearing a WRNS hat, standing at the salute on deck, with all available electric torches shining on him.

This particular company was accommodated by the Navy in HMS *Turtle* at Poole. Throughout the subsequent course of the war a lifebelt hung outside the company office bearing the inscription 'HMS *Mock Turtle*'. It was in their mess, too, that a party was held to celebrate the 50th birthday of the Company Commander and the 21st birthday of his junior subaltern.

Having regard to the difficulty of obtaining sufficient tugs from the Navy to tow the Bigbobs to their moorings, it was decided to experiment with the use of small motorised landing craft, such as LCPs and LCVs manned by Royal Marines. These could be tied alongside the Bigbobs and used to manoeuvre them to their buoys, if these were in sheltered waters. Accordingly four LCPs attached to 141 Flotilla Royal Marines were dispatched from Shoreham, each having a small crew and a Leading Seaman as coxswain. In overall charge was Petty Officer Motor Mechanic E R 'Sandy' Saunders, who graphically described his voyage to Beaulieu:

> We left Shoreham at 7 a.m. on a stormy and overcast morning, wondering what on earth it was we had to do. Each craft had a small tent and other camping equipment, together

with a supply of bread, margarine and corned beef. Then the engine of one of the LCPs seized solid and I was taken alongside to investigate. Jumping aboard was quite hazardous with that sea running and I remember a wag of a stoker shouting out, "You'll do it in two, Chief!" We had to take the crippled craft in tow and seemed to be making little headway. Checking our sailing instructions and chart it appeared that the River Beaulieu was our destination, we were supposed to arrive at the mouth of the estuary to coincide with the high tide (Southampton Water has two tides) at about 2200 hrs. However, the sea was very rough and soaked to the skin, we were only making about three knots and knew we would never make it. At midnight, in the pitch darkness, we knew we must be near the estuary, but by now the tide was running out fast and one of the craft got stuck in the mud. Things were getting pretty desperate and then I saw about a mile away a tiny chink of light which we headed for. Ultimately, we came alongside what turned out to be a mud-dredger of all things! After shouting and banging on its rusty sides for some time, we were hailed from the darkness above, and we asked for directions to Beaulieu River. Following a line of poles fixed in the mud, we eventually found deep water and entered the mouth of the river. The moon came out and we could see where we were going at last – and then well up the river we could see a line of moored ships. 'LCTs,' we shouted and, as we came nearer, we expected to be hailed. We noticed that there seemed to be no sign of life, although we could see them clearly in the moonlight. We went alongside the first one and saw for the first time that they were floating on empty oil drums. 'They're dummies,' we shouted to the other craft and proceeded up river to a small pier where we were met by a Naval officer, who wanted to know where the blanketyblank we had been. The morning came – a beautiful warm and sunny summer's day – and we found that we were on Baron Rothchild's Estate and his house had been taken over as an HQ. We had the task of towing the dummy landing craft to different locations and, during the day, we had a lovely time stuffing ourselves with fruit from the gardens of the house. At night we were ready to start towing as soon as it was dark and moved the first six craft off Pennington Marsh near Lymington. To be honest I don't know where we moved all the craft, as we visited one creek after another and, with all the secrecy and in darkness, we rarely knew exactly where we had been. There was an AA site in a clearing amongst the trees on the Estate and the Army lads told us that they had orders to fire if the daily German reconnaisance plane came too low over the dummies to have become suspicious. When we moored those LCTs on the trots, however, we used to marvel at how lifelike they were, even at close quarters.

In fact, the marked channel referred to by P.O. Saunders leads in from the Solent to the mouth of the Beaulieu river close by Lepe House. From here the river curves between marshy salt flats in a long westerly reach before narrowing and turning towards Buckler's Hard, which lies about three miles from the sea. On the opposite bank to Buckler's Hard is a beautifully kept estate surrounding Exbury House, an attractive country mansion used during the war as HMS *Mastodon,* the setting for Nevil Shute's novel, *Requiem for a Wren.*

It was a small private pier attached to the Exbury estate which 141 Flotilla had run across during their nocturnal adventure. This reach of the river was used throughout the war for a number of clandestine projects and, during the run up to D-day, served as an important repair base and departure point for tank landing craft and MTBs. Clobb Copse, just downstream from Buckler's Hard, was used for experimental work on concrete floating docks and, subsequently, the building of components for the Mulberry harbour.

P O 'Sandy' Saunders with members of 141 Flotilla, who took part in the Bigbob operation at Buckler's Hard

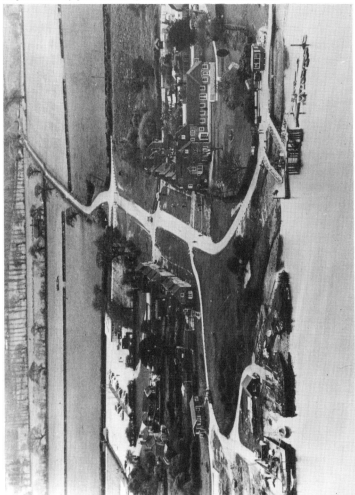

Buckler's Hard, showing the old pier and shipyard. The
Master Builder's House is in the right foreground.

THE STARKEY FIASCO

By the beginning of September, 75 Bigbobs were in position and the Army embarked on an exercise codenamed *Harlequin,* which involved the launching and assembling of 100 or so of the small inflatable dummy assault landing craft (LCAs), known as Wetbobs, in the vicinity of Rye and Richborough on the River Stour. Almost immediately the planners were rewarded by signs of increased aerial activity by enemy reconnaissance planes. Accordingly, it was decided to press ahead with two feint amphibious operations in the English Channel, to be known as *Starkey* and *Wadham,* in order to further compound the enemy confusion. As a setting for these two exercises mock army camps and embarcation points were set up, complete with decoy lighting and the usual deception devices laid on by 'R' force of the Royal Engineers. One of these dummy camps was placed on the Pennington Marshes and the other at Cuckmere Haven, near Seaford. These two sites were selected as being adjacent to the ports of Southampton and Newhaven and simulated wireless traffic was relayed to the Bigbob anchorages using Canadian Army radio trucks.

Meanwhile, a number of beach landing exercises were carried out from Naval establishments in the Portsmouth Command, including Fort Southwick and HMS *Vesting* at Cowes. *Starkey* was scheduled to take place on 8th September and it was intended that it should coincide with the launch of Wetbobs during *Harlequin.* Unfortunately, the weather was bad and a combination of high winds and rough seas played havoc with the light rubber inflatables. As the day of the exercise drew near a note of despair can be detected creeping into the reports of the site commanders:

MOST SECRET

Subject: Wetbobs

Rye

4 September. Owing to wind Navy were unable to tow away to berths. The devices were therefore deflated and repacked.

5 September. 6 of the original 8 Wetbobs berthed were wrecked by the wind and tide.

6 September. No construction or berthing attempted as Navy reported wind too strong for operations.

Richborough

4 September. Military party working from a skiff 'topped-up' devices. Wetbobs were berthed on the trot principle and located on three separate sites.

5 September. Balance of Wetbobs berthed by 0400 hrs. By 1430 hrs 17 were completely wrecked by the wind and tide. Navy collected the remaining 7 into one berth.

6 September. By 0700 hrs remaining 7 Wetbobs capsized by wind or smashed by tide. Day spent in endeavour to salvage wrecks made extremely difficult because of the waterlogged condition and inaccessibility.

Note: Probably due to lack of pre-instruction, the Naval party had little understanding of the peculiarities of Wetbobs and therefore their work was not very satisfactory.

Eventually the weather eased and *Starkey* went ahead on 9th September as planned. An hour before dawn a group of Bigbobs, towed by tugs, escorted by two warships, 19 merchant ships and a mixed assortment of MTBs and landing barges filled with troops, steamed from Dover towards the French coast under an umbrella of 72 fighter aircraft. Simultaneously, aircraft of Bomber Command attacked enemy coastal batteries and airfields in the vicinity of Calais. However, the Germans refused to be drawn and, after heaving-to for some time, the dispirited fleet turned and made for home.

Harlequin was, somewhat thankfully, wound up on the same day in an air of gloom and despondency and *Wadham*, the projected follow-up operation against the Brittany coast, was abandoned soon afterwards.

A week after the *Starkey* fiasco Colonel White made a full report on the Bigbob operation to date 'to help others who may have to carry out the same or similar operation in the future'. His recommendations were to prove invaluable in the planning for *Quicksilver* the following year. He opens with a brief description of the dummy craft and their role:

Bigbobs were dummy LCTs Mk 2, designed to deceive the enemy from high vertical photographs. They were not designed to be proof against low obliques or close ground observation. They were launched at various ports on the South coast to simulate a fleet of craft up the coast. The material was brought to the sites by road, each Bigbob requiring 6 3-ton lorries. These were loaded according to a loading table which was worked out on the first day at Virginia Water.

In future the canvas pieces might have hooks
or clips on two sides and lacings on the
opposite two. This would reduce the time and
labour in lacing. Some form of fender should
be incorporated into the design. The ordinary
rope fender is useless.

The operations at Virginia Water came in for
special comment:

The first week was spent in learning the
various pieces and where they fitted in to
the structure. Modifications were, moreover,
made by the makers during this period. No
drill existed, this had to be evolved in the
first week and was modified as the result of
further experience. It was not until the
second week that the real building began.
However, thanks to the assistance given by
Lieut Allen, RA, and the NCOs from the
Camouflage Establishment, the Officers and
NCOs learnt quickly. I would here like to
stress the very happy relations which existed
between British and American detachments
and the way in which each party was, at all
times, out to help the other.

Virginia Water was a good training site, once
the level of water had been raised
sufficiently. It did not allow for practice
launchings under operational conditions and
in conjunction with the Navy. It would have
been invaluable if the Naval officers
concerned could have seen the prototype at
Virginia Water and so realised sooner what
their problem was and thus have had more
time to prepare plans for the launchings.

The problem of adequate security was also dealt
with at some length:

Local ground security was arranged by the
Command HQs concerned. It was carried out

by the Corps of Military Police with good
and close co-operation of the local civilian
police.

There was, at Poole and Beaulieu, a conflict
between the best sites from the building and
from the security points of view. I decided
that building must have priority if any
programme was to be carried out. It is for
consideration whether, in future, the ground
security should be given more consideration
in the early planning stages, in which case
a slower output might have to be accepted.
I believe that no serious leakage of
information occurred, although a number of
people saw the erection in the early stages
and, I believe, eventually realised what was
being done. In this connection I strongly
recommend that the finished devices should
not be anchored within sight of the building
sites. At Poole it was not very difficult to
connect the activity on the Naval hard with
a sudden increase of LCTs lying, in some
cases, only a few hundred yards away in Poole
Harbour, opposite the Hard.

Small modifications might in future be made
to Bigbobs to make them less conspicuous
from ground observation, e.g. visible parts
of the steelwork to be painted grey, ensigns
to be provided, letters painted on their bows,
possibly some disruptive painting.

At this stage it was decided to dismantle all
the Bigbobs which had been used in the summer
exercises and store them in Cox's 'quarry' at
Watford, a special RAOC depot, which had been
set up for this purpose.

With the co-operation of the Naval officers at
the mooring sites, recovery was started at once.
The craft were winched ashore, using either 30 cwt

trucks or Matador tank recovery vehicles. It was found possible to recover up to six craft each night, although there were a number of problems due to the wheeled undercarriages having rusted up or jammed after being immersed for several weeks in sea water. At Poole the craft were readily pulled up the concrete ramp which had been used for launching. A Matador driving forward was used rather than the winch, but it was found possible only to handle four each night, owing to the small dimensions of the hard. Also tide and wind proved more troublesome than during the launching process because the ships had to be held bows-on to the shore for several minutes while tow ropes were fixed to the Matador.

Although six craft a night were dismantled at Chichester there were many difficulties due to the gentle shelving of the beach. The winch from a Matador parked well above the tide mark had to be used, as the heavy vehicle itself could not be used on the soft sand. The front wheels of the Big-bobs tended to dig into the beach while the stern was still waterborne. Any sideways movement of the floating part due to wind or tide tended to tip the trolleys over on their side. If this happened they had to be dragged in by brute force with the wheels ploughing through the sand.

Since Beaulieu was an inland site there were fewer problems. The craft were pulled ashore using the winch on a 30 cwt lorry parked in a field close by the river. Some of the wheels had rusted badly and would hardly turn, consequently they tended to cut into the turf. Nevertheless, the lorry winch was found to be quite adequate. Because of the current in the river and the need to carefully align the craft to get them through the entrance to the field it was found necessary to attach bow lines and stern lines from the two piers at the site.

Lights on shore were then used as transit marks to keep the correct approach angle.

The time taken to break the craft down into unrecognisable pieces after recovery was about 3-4 hours. Overall damage was negligible. Apart from several wrecked trolley assemblies and consequent damage to some of the lower tubes of the main cantilever frame, the main casualties were the large bow door sections and tie rods. These were often broken or bent by bumping against the tugs whilst still being towed to the beach. Inevitably there was also some damage to the canvas envelope due to tearing or splitting during recovery and dismantling.

As soon as they had been broken down, the Big-bob parts were loaded on lorries and driven to the nearest railhead and transferred to open railway wagons. All these loading operations were carried out by the Pioneer Corps companies who had made up the construction teams, in view of their experience in handling the dummies. After some experimentation it was found possible to load the parts of one complete craft into five wagons. Through trains were used to avoid possible damage due to shunting or trans-shipment. The drivers and guards concerned were also told of the fragile nature of their loads.

The main difficulty encountered was in connection with the large prefabricated gate sections which tended to overhang the sides of the wagons and could foul obstructions, such as tunnels or bridges. Another unforseen problem was that the funnels were likely to become airborne when the train was travelling at speed! Eventually all the dismantled craft arrived at the RAOC storage depots by 25th September and were cleaned and laid up for future use.

Colonel White sent a secret report to COSSAC

Lt Col Peter White, OBE, Commanding Officer, 24 Airfield Construction Group, RE. Responsible for the Bigbob operations at Virginia Water and Beaulieu, 1943

on completion of the operation in which he bitterly criticised the lack of co-ordination between Naval and Army Commands.

MOST SECRET On dismantling Bigbobs
To: COSSAC
ORDERS FOR DISMANTLING
My Company Commanders acted entirely on their own initiative on the verbal information given them by the respective NCOs in charge. Had they not done so the programme which eventually reached them would not have been carried out. I suggest that this again shows the urgent necessity for a Commander for an operation of this sort to which I drew attention in my report forwarded under my 24 ACG/103/1200 dated 1st September, 1943. The Naval programme which was initiated on or about 9th September did not reach the companies who were actually doing the work, through 'normal channels' until about 14th September, i.e. four days after the work had started.

Hothfield Camp   (SGD) P White LtCol RE
Hothfield Common   CRE, 24 Airfield
Nr Ashford, Kent   Construction
                      Group RE

27th September, 1943
During the course of the following month Colonel White held several de-briefing sessions with his Company Commanders concerning the whole Bigbob operation. At a meeting on the morning of 22nd October Major Lewis was asked to produce a detailed Bigbob construction drill for use in possible future operations. The resulting document, which was on Peter White's desk by the evening of the same day, was to prove invaluable

in the run-up to 'Operation *Quicksilver*' the following year.

The basic plan was quite simple. A senior NCO was placed in charge of each device and had under him two teams of one NCO and nine men each, known as the 'Bow Party' and the 'Stern Party' respectively. Building of the 'boat' was started in the middle between bays No.10 and 11, which were erected on stands. The two teams worked away from each other, fitting together the sub assemblies until they reached the bow and stern. One of the team was responsible for fitting the floats and trolleys as the work progressed. When the main cantilever frame was completed the bow door and superstructure were fitted, while the 'Stern Party' erected the funnel. The canvas and camouflage were laid out under the respective bays until darkness. Complete silence was insisted upon throughout the entire operation and the ships were launched stern first to avoid damage.

Low level photograph of Bigbobs moored in the River Beaulieu to check on their appearance at close quarters
Reproduced by permission of the Public Record Office

ARMY FORM C2136 (Small)

MESSAGE FORM

IMPORTANT

| Call | Srl. No. | Priority | | Register No. | D |

ABOVE THIS LINE FOR SIGNALS USE ONLY

Transmission Instructions

Office Date & time

FROM (A)   EXFOR

Originator   P

For Action   Date-Time of Origin   221600

HOFOR

TO

(W) For Information (INFO)

Message Instructions   QQY

MOST SECRET

O(D)5. MOST SECRET. PLEASE REQUEST O.C. UNITS NOMINATED FOR

TRG IN DUMMY CRAFT TO ATTEND CONFERENCE THIS HQ AT HIGH HOUS

BROOK GREEN 1600 HRS 25 JAN.

This message will not be distributed

| THIS MESSAGE MAY BE SENT AS WRITTEN | IF LIABLE TO BE INTERCEPTED OR TO FALL INTO ENEMY HANDS, THIS MESSAGE MUST BE SENT IN CIPHER | ORIGINATOR'S INSTRUCTIONS DEGREE OF PRIORITY |
| BY ANY MEANS { EXCEPT { WIRELESS | | P |

SIGNED

O.T.P. need not be paraphrased),

ORIGINATOR'S INSTRUCTIONS

Time   System

THRO' TOR

Time cleared

OPERATION QUICKSILVER

Despite the failure of *Starkey* and *Wadham*, the ever dynamic John Bevan and his American counterpart, Colonel Baumer, were already working on another massive deception plan, which had been code-named *Fortitude*. This was to be part of the background to operation *Overlord*, the invasion of Europe by Allied forces in June, 1944. By the end of December, 1943, the details of *Fortitude* had been worked out and approved by the Commanders-in-Chief and the Prime Minister, Winston Churchill.

Early in January, 1944, Bevan flew to Moscow to explain the plans to the Russians. The operation covered four theatres of war. *Fortitude* S was to be a feint attack on the Pas de Calais coastal strip and *Fortitude* N a similar operation against the coast of Norway. *Zeppelin* was a deception plan for the Eastern Mediterranean, based on a dummy fleet of 100 landing craft at Tobruk, and *Ironside* and *Vendetta* were similar exercises to be mounted in the Western Mediterranean.

The tactical component of *Fortitude S*, which was to be carried out on D-day itself, included the use of dummy paratroopers in gliders, simulated assaults on Fécamp and Boulogne and the use of silver foil dropped from aircraft to confuse enemy radar. The strategic counterpart of the plan was to be mounted as soon as possible and was to be known as *Quicksilver*.

The object of this exercise was to mislead the
Germans as to the area selected by the Allies for
the invasion of Europe and to convince them **after**
D-day that the Normandy landings were simply a
ruse to draw attention away from the Pas de
Calais. The latter region was already considered
by the German Commander-in-Chief, General von
Runstedt, to be highly likely as the prime target
of the invasion spearhead for a number of reasons.
It was the shortest sea route from England and
close to a number of French deepwater ports. Also
it was within striking distance of the 'V' bomb sites
and the industrial Ruhr in Germany. To encourage
this view, a large fleet of dummy landing craft was
to be moored around the South-eastern and Eastern
Coast from Yarmouth to Folkestone during the
weeks immediately preceeding D-day, and bombing
of the Pas de Calais area intensified.

It was estimated that an additional hundred
Bigbobs would be required, which would be
constructed to simulate the new Mark 4 LCTs.
Together with the dummy craft already available,
this would give a total fleet of 315 craft.
Consequently, orders were placed with Cox's of
Watford on 1st December for the additional craft
to be delivered by 1st March the following year.

Although it was decided that dummy LCAs
(Wetbobs) would also be included in the *Quicksilver*
plan it was thought doubtful if these would be
suitable for any long term use. The inflatable kind
which had been used in *Starkey* had not stood
up well to wind and tide and efforts were made
to modify their design to make them more rigid
and of stronger material. Some 160 of the original
Wetbobs were still usable and it was decided that
with an additional 150 of the new rigid pattern the
COSSAC requirements would be safely met. It was
also planned to use 36 specially modified Bigbobs,

which would appear as obvious dummies. These could be used as a double bluff decoy at selected moorings and then quickly converted back to the standard form when needed. Comparative photographic tests were to be carried out between obvious dummies, good dummies and real craft to confirm their effectiveness.

To complement this phantom fleet a phantom army was to be created by simulating a build-up of British, Canadian and American troops in the same South-eastern corner of the United Kingdom. Mock army camps with acres of tents and smoking field kitchens, huge dumps of empty Jerry-cans and ammunition boxes, camouflaged lines of dummy tanks and guns, and make-believe radio traffic to and from the fictitious 1st United States Army Group (FUSAG) all helped to create the illusion. A fake HQ for Montgomery's 21st Army Group was set up deep in the Kent countryside, while the real headquarters was in Portsmouth. All messages were relayed to the fake HQ by telephone and then relayed from there by radio for the benefit of the German listening posts on the continent.

At Dover three miles of the foreshore were cleared to build a fake oil depot. This was shelled several times by the German batteries on Cap Gris Nez and hits were shammed using sodium flares and fires of waste sump oil and old rubber tyres.

All these operations were designed to be revealed to the enemy by 'neglect of concealment', while the real preparations for *Overlord* in the South and South-west of the country were kept hidden as far as possible.

On the afternoon of 25th January, 1944, a meeting of the officers commanding units earmarked for training in the *Quicksilver* operation was held at High House, Brook Green,

47

Woolverstone Hall

Ness Farm above the River Stour, almost opposite
Parkeston Quay. One of the sites originally considered
for the building of Bigbobs in 1944

Hammersmith, which was then the 21st Army Group's London HQ. Amongst other things, it was decided to immediately set up a training camp for the instruction of Bigbob construction teams, to be situated somewhere in East Anglia, preferably close to the Naval base at Harwich.

The sites considered were Ness Farm on the River Orwell, the foreshore adjacent to Felixstoweferry near Felixstowe, Freston Park on the River Orwell, and Waldringfield on the River Deben. Waldringfield was a small village within easy reach of Ipswich much used by amateur yachtsmen during peacetime and was finally selected as the ideal spot for Bigbob training.

Within a fortnight a small team of officers and men who had been involved in the previous Bigbob exercises were appointed as instructors and supervised the preparation of the site, under the direction of Captain Allen, RE, the chief instructor. Several beach huts on the river bank were demolished, a field known locally as Sedge Close at the back of the parish church was cleared as a construction site, and a slipway 200 yards by 50 yards was levelled down to the river.

The component parts for building two Bigbobs were then delivered to the site from Cox's factory and the usual strict security precautions were put into effect around the village and its immediate surroundings. On 14th February twenty officers and forty senior NCOs from the 10th Battalion, Worcestershire Regiment, and the 4th Battalion, Northamptonshires, began their training in erecting and launching the 5-ton dummies. The men were billeted in the village, the old Maltings and Mrs Turner's Guest House being used by the officers. The only pub in the village was the Maybush and this received extra rations of beer for the benefit of the troops in training. Albert and Grace Hill, licencees of the Maybush for 31 years, remember the time well, although Albert spent most of the war as a Petty Officer in the Navy at HMS *Beehive*, an MTB repair base at nearby Felixstowe.

By the end of the course three weeks later the group had achieved the creditable time of just over six hours from the commencement of building until the final mooring in the river, the whole operation being carried out in darkness. A modification of Max Lewis' original construction drill was eventually worked out as a result of these early trials. Three teams were used for each craft; building the bow section, midship section and stern respectively. After the sections had been bolted together the teams added the superstructure funnel and mast, fixed the bow doors and covered the skeleton with painted canvas sheets, which were laced to the frames. The finished craft were run down the slipway on their wheeled undercarriages and then floated off into the river, where they were taken in tow to their mooring buoys.

Further assemblies were now arriving at the site from Cox's and these were stored under hedges, covered by camouflage netting. The personnel selected for the first course were now used as instructors, in turn, for the second group of 150 other ranks, who arrived at Waldringfield on 15th March. Two further courses were run during March and early April, by which time a total force of 700 men had received training. As there were no facilities on site the men were billeted during their stay at quarters in Ipswich.

Because the diversionary Bigbob programme was to stretch along the coast from Great Yarmouth to Folkestone and the real preparations for *Overlord* were taking place along the South and South-west seaboard, it was decided on 1st April, 1944, to seal off a coastal strip, 1 mile deep, from the Wash to Land's End. This security measure was enforced until 15th August, by which time the European bridgehead had been firmly established.

The officer appointed to mastermind the *Quicksilver* operation was Colonel David Strangeways, who was on the staff of COSSAC. Strangeways was given wide powers to ensure that the operation ran to schedule and was responsible directly to the C-in-C, 21st Army Group. On 2nd April he sent a detailed plan to the field commanders and Naval officers involved, designating the build-and-launch sites for the Bigbobs, selected after secret recces carried out during the previous two months.

Waldringfield was to be retained as a site, together with new locations at Great Yarmouth, Lowestoft, Woolverstone Park (near Ipswich), Dover and Folkestone. Numbers of craft to be launched at each site and the launching and berthing areas were also described.

A special problem at Dover was that the beach and harbour could be overlooked from the cliffs above. Lieutenant A W Lyons of the RE special 'R' deception unit recalls, 'It would have been impossible to deceive spies with the dummy landing craft, as they could have overlooked the harbour from the cliffs. So large screens were erected to prevent this, while still indicating that 'something was going on'. I gathered that the steel and canvas LCTs were to mislead aerial observation and remember that they were constructed on the beaches. The Engineers laid tracks down the beaches to the 'loading bays' at the water's edge. Roads to the port were strengthened and sometimes re-surfaced, corners concreted and widened for tank turnings and roads signposted towards the coast to give the impression that preparations were afoot for an influx of armoured and other vehicles **prior to embarcation. Deception** areas were also constructed for all types of Assembly Point, e.g. RASC, REME, etc. At night, noises were heard of tanks moving along the roads, truck engines, construction work and many other forms of deception, such as wireless traffic passing between the various 'ghost' units'.

The launching hard at Dover was situated on the beach below the Castle and some of the houses in the immediate area were evacuated as a security precaution. Also a number of beach huts had to be demolished and many tons of chalk cleared away. The Navy, meantime, laid several trots of mooring buoys in the harbour, where the Bigbobs could tie up. Folkestone Harbour was similarly buoyed and the beach to the east of the fish market used for building purposes. The HQ and Support Company of the Worcesters was deployed at Dover, while 'B' Company was sent to Folkestone. The Northamptonshires were deployed at Great Yarmouth and Lowestoft.

The largest building programme took place in Suffolk on the Rivers Orwell and Deben, which run roughly parallel courses to the sea from Ipswich and Woodbridge. 'A' Company of the Worcesters was deployed at Woolverstone Park on the Orwell, while 'C' and 'D' Companies were based on the training site at Waldringfield.

Real LCT Mark IV's being used during the landings in Sicily, 10 July, 1943 (Operation Husky)

THE BLUFF SUCCEEDS

Towards the end of May, convoys of lorries moved out of the RASC depot at Boreham Wood to load up with Bigbob components from Cox's storage dumps. Sections of seven 3-ton lorries (6 covered and one open) were used for each complete assembly 'kit' and these were escorted to the various building sites by an Army motorcycle dispatch rider. Howard Wilton, the works manager at Cox's, recollects that the sight of several hundred lorries pouring out of the factory gates and on to the Watford by-pass prompted much speculation amongst the watching locals.

Mr R J Noyce, a driver in one of these convoys whilst serving in the RASC, recalls journeying to Woolverstone Park during May, 1944:

Our job was to transport materials used in the construction of the dummy LCTs to the sites near Ipswich and Dover. The section would report to the Ordnance Depot and the vehicles loaded with the necessary material, which consisted mainly of large empty oil drums, canvas and metal tubing similar to that used for scaffolding. The following day the section would proceed in convoy to the site. To the best of my recollection the final

stage of the route to the site on the River
Orwell, near Ipswich, was via country lanes
and eventually ended in a wooded area. Here
the lorries were unloaded and the contents
placed out of sight under the hedgerows in
the woods. I am unable to given any details
as to the actual construction of the dummy
LCTs, because this always took place at night
while I was asleep in the back of one of the
vehicles. In the morning the completed LCT
would be afloat and all that could be seen
was a Jeep towing a harrow over the field
to erase all tell-tale tracks and evidence of
the previous night's activity. At Dover the
LCTs were constructed on the waterfront
and I remember that huge camouflage nets
were hung across some roads leading down
to the harbour. The completed LCTs were
indistinguishable from the real thing at 25
yards.
Although the first Bigbobs were launched at
Yarmouth on 20th May, work did not start on the
Deben and Orwell sites until some days later. The
Woolverstone site was delightfully situated in the
park surrounding the old Hall, which was built in
1776, as the country seat of the Berners family.
The construction area was in an expanse of open
parkland bounded by a line of trees close to the
river bank, where the ground sloped steeply down
to the water. The Worcesters were encamped in
tents in an adjoining part of the park which held
a small church formerly used by the family and
their servants. The site was ideal for the Bigbob
operation, because the trees bordering the building
area could be used for concealing the assembly
material until required.
Further, a roadway, cut through the trees, led
down to a cobbled hard on the river bank, at the

centre of which a small pier ran out to the deep water channel, which was dredged to a depth of 20 feet to enable small coastal vessels and colliers to sail up-river to Ipswich. This provided ample room for the dummies to be moored at trots of buoys laid in the wide sweep of the River Orwell from Woolverstone to Pin Mill, known as Potter's Reach. One of the few houses facing the river at this point was the historic Cat House, so called because in the days of smuggling the silhouette of a cat was placed in the parlour window as an all-clear signal.

During the War the Hall itself was used by the Navy and Royal Marines as a 'stone frigate', HMS *Woolverstone,* at this time under the command of Captain J C Mansfield, RN. The Hall housed a signal and coding section manned by WRNS and was used as an administrative centre for the personnel engaged on *Quicksilver.* Officers were billeted in the Hall, whilst other ranks were housed in Nissen huts built in the gardens behind the main buildings. The old stables at the side of the Hall were used for stores and equipment and the Royal Marines of 446 Flotilla, under the command of Captain Marsh, RM, were accommodated in tents pitched just outside the main gates leading to the rose garden.

The wooded land alongside the Orwell, leading to Pin Mill, was used to simulate an Army encampment complete with guard house, parade square, tents and the now-familiar range of dummy equipment, 'night noises', phantom convoys of army lorries, and wireless traffic to 21st Army Group HQ. Later, as the number of Bigbobs mounted in the river, fake wireless messages were also passed from ship to shore, concerning the usual range of matters such as provisions, medical supplies, Fleet Notices, ammunition and damage reports.

The build-and-launch programme started at Woolverstone on 22nd May and, although there was little moonlight, the weather remained fairly calm and dry. This enabled the target of four launches each night to be maintained without any serious hitches. The Worcestershires soon became highly skilled at working in almost complete darkness and with hardly a spoken word. They used the 3-team method perfected at Waldringfield, the canvas, superstructure, funnel, bow doors and bridge being added just before launch. Even coils of rope on the decks and an ensign and halyards for the mast were not forgotten.

The vehicle hold was covered with camouflage netting poked up from below by wooden poles lashed to the metal framework to simulate the outlines of tanks and lorries. As each craft was finished it was manhandled off the construction site and down the slipway to the hard on the iron-wheeled undercarriages welded below the flotation tanks. During the launch the articulated nature of the Bigbob framework enabled the bow and centre section to float off horizontally, while the stern was still on the sloping hard. At this point the Royal Marines took over from the Army and attached pairs of small landing craft (LCVs and LCPs) to the sides of the dummies, using hand lines. With a final heave from the men ashore, the Bigbobs were then towed off the hard and out into deep water by the RM coxswains manning the 'tugs'. Operations were co-ordinated from the Bigbob bridge by a Naval officer perilously perched some 20 feet above the water, standing on a length of duckboard lashed to the craft framework.

Two Naval officers had been attached to 446 Flotilla RM as boat officers for this purpose, one being the author of this narrative and the other a commissioned Bo'sun known affectionately as

View of part of the Bigbob mooring area in Potter's
Reach from the hard at Woolverston

The Butt & Oyster on the Orwell, just below Woolverston
- a favourite haunt of the Quicksilver teams. A 'butt'
is a local name for a flounder

'Darby' Allen. The manoeuvring and mooring of the Bigbobs at night was quite a delicate process, because their lack of draught and high canvas sides made them difficult to handle if there was more than a breath of wind or if the tide was running strongly. After slowly edging down-stream to Potter's Reach, the craft were tied up fore and aft in pairs to small orange yacht buoys laid some 70 yards apart. Extreme care had to be taken at this stage to avoid damage to the Bigbobs by grounding either on the river bank or one of the numerous mud banks. Because of the articulated nature of the main frame to run aground would distort the ship in such a way that it would almost certainly reveal it to be a dummy if photographed by enemy reconnaissance aircraft. In the same way, any dummy craft which could not be launched and moored during the hours of darkness had to be dismantled and returned to camouflaged storage before day-break.

As in all these operations strict security measures were taken to prevent unauthorised movements to and from the Woolverstone site. The effectiveness of these measures was demonstrated by the following incident. One evening the liaison officer of the Worcesters, Lieut. 'Wattie' Watkins, and the author decided to 'break out' of camp and visit the Butt & Oyster at Pin Mill for a convivial pint of bitter. The outward journey through a hole in the boundary hedge and along a deserted footpath skirting the river was uneventful. On retracing our steps, however, we were pounced upon, as we climbed back through the hedge, by an armed Naval patrol which was laying in wait for us. An alert sentry had spotted us leaving an hour or so previously and had alerted the guardroom. Fortunately the Provost-Marshal was in a good mood and we were released after a friendly warning.

By D-day on 6th June, 50 Bigbobs were safely moored in the Orwell without casualty and a further 20 vessels were added during the following week. A large fleet of some 300 dummy LCTs were now distributed along the East and South-east seaboard from Great Yarmouth to Folkestone. The craft were animated by the construction crews, who used numerous ingenious dodges and devices.

These proved so successful that even the WRNS at HMS *Woolverstone* had no idea that the Bigbobs were other than real craft. The White Ensign was flown at the masts of all the dummies during the hours of daylight, while skeleton crews moved about the decks carrying out imaginary tasks or even fishing over the sides. Items of laundered clothing were hung out to dry and signalling between ship and shore was carried out by Aldis lamp. Specially designed oil burners were located inside the funnels to produce intermittent plumes of smoke and men were slung over the sides in cradles to 'paint ship'.

Regular small boat services called at each Bigbob in turn and delivered mail bags, ammunition boxes and other ships' stores. 'Liberty boats' also called at intervals to take men ashore and return them at appropriate intervals. Small tankers also steamed around the fleet tying up alongside craft and laying out oiling hoses to simulate re-fuelling operations. The mooring patterns of the craft were also varied from time to time and the numbers of ships altered by regular sailings of real LCTs, which mingled with the dummies.

Enemy reconnaissance aircraft regularly over-flew the mooring sites at high altitude. These were fired upon by local AA batteries to avoid suspicion, but the gunners were told that under no circumstances were the planes to be brought down, as it was essential that photographs of the dummy fleet reached German Intelligence. The effectiveness of this ploy was demonstrated when the Cap Gris Nez shore batteries shelled the Bigbobs at Dover and Folkestone. The dummy craft bore this attack amazingly well and several which had been damaged and set adrift refused to sink. Eventually they had to be chased and disposed of by puncturing their flotation tanks and scuttling them. After this episode the German radio broadcast to Britain boasted that severe damage had been caused to the fleet and the Allied invasion forces had been held off indefinitely. Needless to say, the gunners themselves had to suffer in silence a lot of leg-pulling by the locals about the accuracy of their shooting.

Meanwhile the tactical component of *Fortitude S* had also proved effective in confusing the Germans. Enemy radar was rendered virtually useless by the massive use of 'Mandrel', a highly efficient jamming device carried by a force of 29 Lancaster bombers, known as the *ABC Patrol,* flying back and forth along the enemy invasion coast. The jamming was reinforced by another squadron of bombers, led by Group Captain Leonard Cheshire, VC, dropping bundles of metal foil strips (Window) at one minute intervals to produce misleading echoes on the enemy radar screens.

Two feint attacks were also made on Channel coastal areas to create the impression of additional landings and draw attention away from Normandy. In Operation *Taxable* a small fleet of motor launches (MLs) from Portsmouth, sailing at convoy speed, steamed towards Cap d'Antibes towing strings of low-flying balloons fitted with radar reflecting devices. *Glimmer* was a similar operation carried out by MLs from Dover against possible landing beaches around Boulogne.

The Maltings at Waldringfield, operational HQ for the units of the 10th Worcesters and 4th Northants in training for Quicksilver

Cat House Hard and jetty below HMS Woolverston on the River Orwell

Simultaneously, in operation *Titanic,* hundreds of dummy uniformed parachutists, fitted with self-detonating fireworks to simulate rifle fire, were dropped at Yvetot, about 20 miles inland from Le Havre and Dieppe. Other drops were made between St Lô and Caen, at the base of the Cherbourg Peninsular.

Even after the invasion of Europe had taken place the *Quicksilver* deception continued to play an important role. On 10th June (D+4) General Guingand, 21st Army Group Chief-of-Staff, signalled to Colonel Wills, commanding the 10th Worcesters, as follows:

> The Chief-of-Staff is anxious that the threat created to N. France by the dummy landing craft under your control be continued as long as possible. It is during the next fortnight that we may well obtain most benefit from these craft. While it is realised that the launching and maintenance of the craft is an extremely arduous task it is requested that every possible effort be made to ensure that as much life and animation is given to them as possible. You should explain to all ranks that they are playing an extremely important part in the plan, and that in view of this they are required to make as great an effort as battalions deployed in the battle area.

The maintenance of the dummy fleets was especially difficult where they were moored at sea, directly exposed to the effects of wind and weather. As June drew to a close the weather deteriorated along the Channel coast and on 2nd July Colonel Wills sent an urgent signal to GHQ SE Command:

> Cannot keep Bigbob fleet afloat at Dover without tug or powerful craft of not less than 50 hp and 4' draught. Bad weather and high

winds bring serious troubles and the efforts of 200 officers and men to keep craft in good order can be nullified in a few hours unless a powerful vessel under my orders is at short notice by day or night to retrieve dummies broken from moorings or to bring in craft damaged beyond repair for stripping down and rebuilding. Proper animation depends upon a very frequent change of mooring and continued movement of small craft to and from the hards.

However, matters were overtaken by events and, within a few days, the decision was made to recover and dismantle the dummy craft which, by then, had achieved their purpose.

Secret files later captured from the Germans by the advancing Allied troops included Intelligence Reports made at the time of the D-day landings, estimating that there were at least 42 divisions of Allied forces and a fleet of 500 large landing craft massed in southeast England, poised for a major invasion attempt in the Pas de Calais region. In reality only 15 divisions were being held in reserve and there were no ships.

The *Quicksilver* operation tied down a large number of German troops in the area to the northeast of the Normandy beaches around Fécamp, Boulogne and Dieppe. These included several Panzer divisions of the 14th and 15th German armies. The absence of these forces from the fierce tank battles around Caen facilitated the breakout of the Allied armies and the early capture of the deep water port of Cherbourg on 26th June which ensured the success of the bridgehead.

The great bluff had succeeded.

Appendix 'A'

"BIGBOB" - PHASE PROGRAMME

	Number to be launched each day							Sailing movements of real LCTs				
	Yarmouth	Lowestoft	River Deben	River Orwell	Dover	Folkestone	BUILD UP	Yar'h/Lowestoft	Yar'h/Deben	Yar'h/Orwell	Debén/Dover	Dover/Folk'n
May 20	4						4					
21	4						8		4			
22	4		4				16		4			
23	4		4				24		4	4		
24			4	4			32	3	4	4	5	
25	4	3	4	4	5		52	3		4		
26	4	3		4			63		4	4	5	
27	4		4	4	5		80	4	4		5	4
28		4	4		5	4	97		4	4		4
29	4		4	4		4	113			4	5	
30	4			4	5		126		4	4	5	4
31	4		4	4	5	4	147		3		5	
June 1	4		3		5		159		3	4	2	2
2	3		3	4	2	2	173	3	3			4
3		3	3			4	183	2	3	4	4	
4	2	2	3	4	4		198		4	4		
5				4	4		206	2	3	4		
6		2	3	4			215	3	3	4		
7		3	3	4			225		3		5	
8			3		5		233		3	4	2	
9			3	4	1		241		2	4		
10			3	4			248			4		
11				4			252			3		
12				3			255					
Total	49	20	59	63	46	18	255					

ACKNOWLEDGEMENTS

Piecing together the complex jigsaw of the Bigbob story has been a lengthy and often frustrating exercise. Now security regulations have been lifted the whole episode can be described for the first time. The trail of information has snaked back and forth across the country and even further afield to Malta and Australia. A number of correspondents, most of whom I have never met, have willingly explored their files and photograph albums and searched their memories to recall events that took place over 40 years ago. Without their help and the co-operation of the Ministry of Defence, the Public Record Office and numerous libraries, museums and local newspapers the story would have remained untold. It is therefore with much pleasure that I record my thanks to all those who have so readily afforded me their time and assistance.

I am especially indebted to John English, Jim Clay and Colonel Peter White for their continuing support and interest, together with my faithful letter-writers, Alex 'Ben' Lyons and 'Sandy' Saunders, who also helped with photographic material. I must also mention the aid of Susan Tomkins, the Heritage Archivist at Beaulieu, which proved invaluable. Others, including the following, have contributed in a number of ways - L Bromhall, Mrs A Bradbury (Windsor Library), P Buckley (MoD Army Historical Branch), Jane Carmichael & Vivienne Crawford (Imperial War Museum), John Cox, A E Crawley, A J Crawley (National Maritime Museum), D Chaston, B Cropper (Watford Central Library), Oliver Green, D J Hawkins (MoD Naval Historical Branch), Col. C T F Holland MBE (RE Museum), David Johnson (Watford Library), R J Noyce, Capt. D Oakley (Globe & Laurel), C R Orr-Ewing (Exbury House), Canon David Strangeways, S Wilson, Jennifer Weller, Howard Wilton, Doreen Williamson (Local Studies Library, Guildford) and the Editors of the *Dover Express* and *Watford Observer* and Philip Scott (Photographic Librarian, Beaulieu).

Crown copyright material in the Public Record Office is reproduced by permission of the Controller of Her Majesty's Stationery Office.

The quotation from Lord Montgomery's *Normandy to the Baltic* is reproduced by permission of A P Watt, Ltd., on behalf of Viscount Montgomery of Alamein.

The short extract from Colonel White's article, 'An Overlord Deception', appearing on page 18 is reproduced by permission of the *Royal Engineers' Journal.*